60 QUOTES FOR SUCCESS

An illustrated book of quotes for Coaching and Mentoring

Dr Sudeendra Koushik

Quotes are very powerful.

So are pictures.

This is a collection of thoughts that came with my experience of coaching and mentoring leaders and professionals in diverse fields and geographies.

I have captured some of the powerful ones which helped me in my coaching and mentoring programs. I have put out some short lines as notes for these thoughts along with an illustration as a context or a guide. Some are intended to make you think, beyond what meets the eye.

Am sure this will give you a chance give your own meaning. And perhaps your own quotes too.

Whether you are coaching or mentoring someone else or yourself, hope this will guide you too in some way.

Dr Sudeendra Koushik,

https://www.linkedin.com/in/sudeendrakoushik/

The best way to kill creativity is by making assumptions

Making assumptions stops us from pursuing certain creative paths, makes us devoid of options. It prevents us from being creative, new possibilities will never be explored. The key is to question as many assumptions as we have, then decide which ones to keep or change.

Confidence and Competence are not the same thing

Confidence comes from the belief you have in yourself. It's a good thing. It helps you manage new and unfamiliar situations. But competence is a different thing, a skill well learnt, with finesse. Confidence can induce forced errors, which could be avoided.

Hard work is about alignment not amount of effort

Some activities seem harder than others. And it is true. The real reason is not because of amount of effort. It is very often due to the alignment of effort to your liking. Though the 'amount' of work remains the same, the choice of work makes it easier. Choose wisely and you will not 'feel' the hard work.

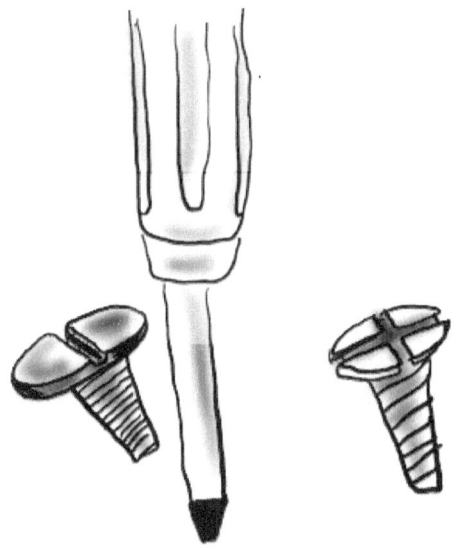

Things don't cease to exist because you don't know

Many things are not known to many of us. Just because I am ignorant about something doesn't mean there is no such thing. Knowing 'I know what I don't know' is the key. Knowing what we don't know is the starting point of learning.

The height of performance is based on the breadth of your understanding and the depth of your reasoning

Reasoning decides what we know and what we don't know. Understanding establishes the relationships and the context of the situation. These are critical inputs for decision making. Decision sets the actions followed by results.

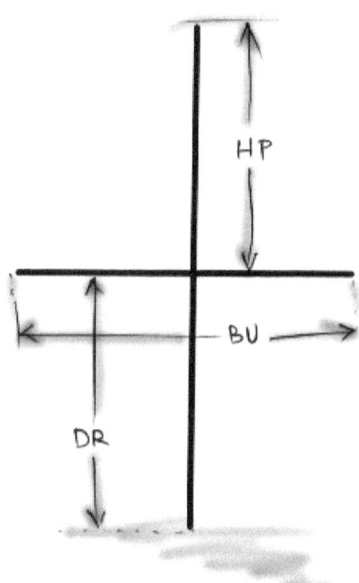

The right question sets the direction right

If we do not know where we are going, then it doesn't matter which road we take. The right question forces us to think why we are doing whatever we are doing. The probability of success is more or less decided, the moment we ask and answer the right question.

Innovation is fun, but not a joke

Creating something new is always exciting and fun.
Innovation creates something but it is very tough to come
up with something new that is useful. A lot of empathy
and effort goes into making this happen. It's no joke.

Your perception of a risk does not change the risk itself

As a person, one can be risk averse or an aggressive risk-taker. This however does not change the actual risk in the real world. What you think about the risk is your perception of the risk. Whatever the risk is remains so.

The ability to argue has nothing to do with the quality of the argument

Many times, the ability to argue makes an impact on the argument. Usually a good debater makes an argument sound much better than it actually is. Talking more is no way better, talking better is no way good. Less can be more here, argument is the key. In cricket we say, to be a good batsman, play the ball not the bowler.

An idea that can defend itself is better

than an idea that needs you to defend

Ideas are the seeds of innovation. While good ideas do not sell themselves, they can surely defend themselves. A good idea does not need to be defended too much. Defending ideas means there is something too good about the idea or something not so good about the idea.

A Good leader is like a movie projector; showing what is ahead while staying behind

A leader has to see what is up next and make plans for the future. This vision sets the direction for the team. A leader should see forward but need not be in the front. He/she should ensure that the team is moving in the right direction, 'have their backs' as they say.

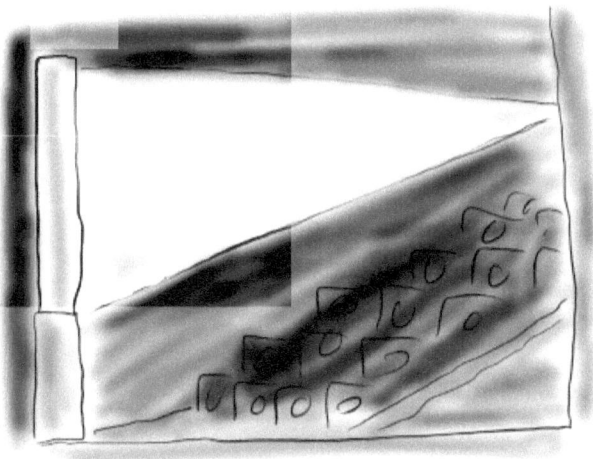

A ladder will not get you to the top

Tools are tools, resources remain as resources. A ladder will not get you to the top. A ladder will help, but in no way will replace your efforts to climb. A ladder can never make the climbing redundant. Climbing up the wall can make the ladder redundant. Plans are necessary. Action remains the key.

The customer is not always 'right', but always has the 'right' to choose

A customer has the right to choose. But this doesn't make his choice right or wrong. Your choice as a maker and his as a customer might be different. Understand this is about choice and not right or wrong.

Professionalism is inversely proportional to the difference between what you say and what you do

Professionalism is doing what you say you promised to do. Professionalism can be mediocre when actions and promises do not match. Do what you say and say what you do. Doing more than promised is less beneficial compared to doing less than promised which is more harmful.

Every idea is a great idea till it is implemented

Ideas are basically conceptual. When a concept hits reality, the conversion from the thought to reality creates hurdles which never seemed to exist. The best test for anything is time. The proof is in the pudding.

Knowledge can get you power, power can never get you knowledge

Knowledge can get you many things, and power is one of them. Power is a force which can never get us knowledge. It is a one-way street. Choose wisely.

I am sure I think I am sure

Looking at life and situations as binary is not always helpful. Simplification is necessary but over-simplification is harmful. Situations are non-binary, not always a yes or no. A scale is a better option to assess than two fixed options. It is ok to do it that way. A scale can be bent.

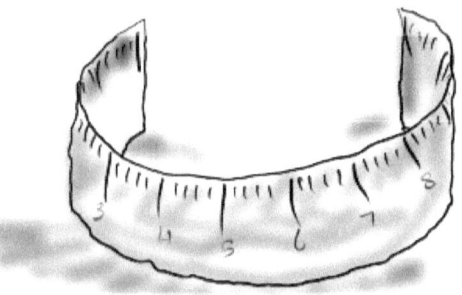

Leadership =
Transfer of ownership +
Retaining accountability

A leader wants to get as much done, and always done with full commitment. This can happen when transfer of ownership is achieved. The team should feel as much as the leader about the work to be done. The leader remains accountable though. Leadership is to inspire not just getting things done.

If you want to be unique, give up being safe

Seeing things from a viewpoint, a unique one takes one to tread unfamiliar paths. Roads are created by some by treading a path. The path was started by the first one who took that non-existent route. Being safe means, you won't create a path, you won't get a unique view. Don't settle for mediocrity.

Discover problems, Invent solutions

Success comes from contributing to opportunities and problems in unique but better ways than existing ways. Real opportunities and problems are to be discovered. New solutions are to be invented. Often, we create problems which do not exist, providing solutions that are not necessary, the real reason why innovation fails. Don't start with a medicine and try to find a disease. Over-thinking is one way to invent problems.

Follow your temperament and not your passion

Following our passion leads us in the direction of what 'we want'. Our temperament tells what we 'can'. How well we perform in a role or job is decided by our temperament. Passion gets us started, temperament keeps us going, or not.

Sweet spot

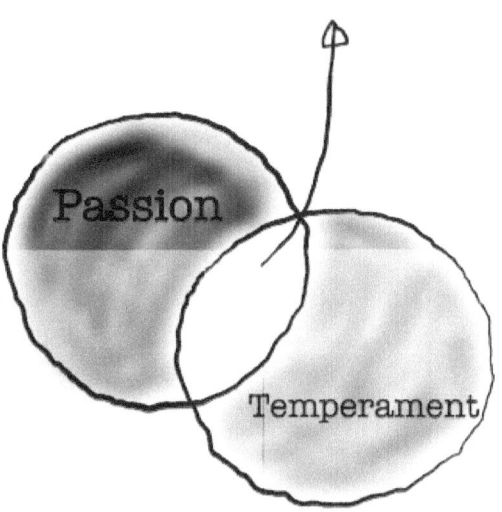

Passion

Temperament

If you love it, you will do it

No matter how tough it is or how inaccessible something is, if we really love something, we will do it. The energy goes towards things we love. The love for something creates the energy draft towards it. Love for something is much stronger than liking something. Next time you find making excuses, check again – like or love.

Intent | Knowledge | Decision | Action | Outcome

If you don't like a 'outcome', check your actions.

If you don't like an 'action', check your Decision.

If you don't like a 'decision', check your knowledge.

If you don't like your 'knowledge', check your intent.

Don't fix a problem that you don't really understand

Any problem has to be really and really understood before acting on it, attempting to solve it. Causality helps understand the cause and effect. Correlation helps understand relationships. Analysis creates confusion of what is the cause and what is the effect. Action bias is good. But timing of action is more important.

If you don't think big,
you will act small

No action will benefit us if we think small. Every action does have an impact on the big picture if we know the big picture. The action need not be big to be impactful. It's the awareness of the connection to the big picture that is necessary for actions to have a big impact. It helps us choose or discard a course of action.

Knowledge is potential power

Knowledge is not power; knowledge does not give results. When actions are based on knowledge it can give good results. Today knowledge is not power as everybody has access to information. But what we do with what we know is the difference. A battery pack is potential power till it is connected to a circuit.

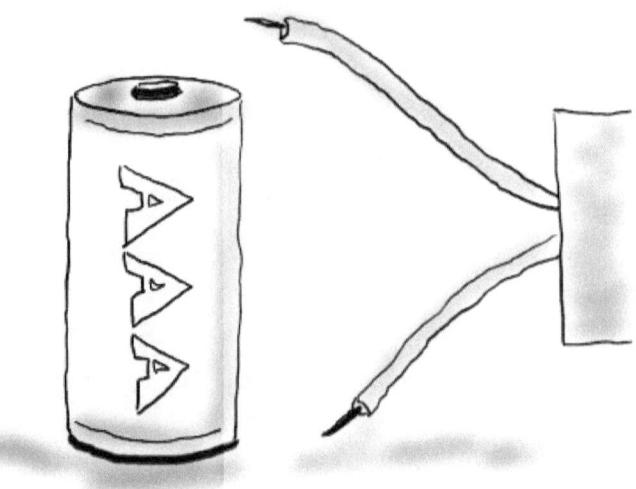

There are only results, no failures

Results are the reasons why we act on most of the things. However, the word failure has led to fear factor and has created havoc in our minds. This prevents many of us from taking action. Failure is another kind of result. The difference between a plan and the outcome is important. Getting what we expected or planned is success. When the result is not as per plan or as expected it is failure. Nothing more, noting less.

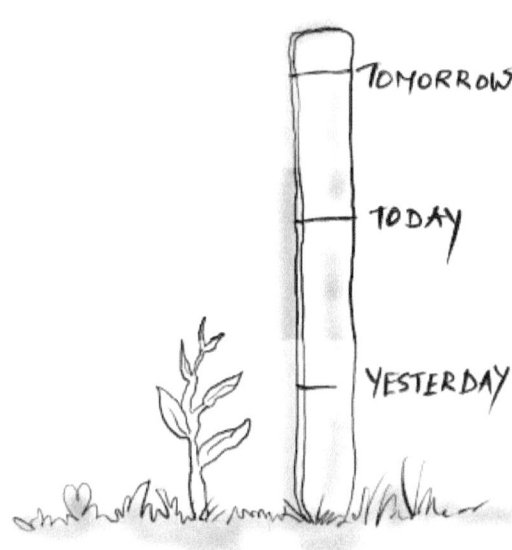

Good leadership is raising the floor

Raising the floor. Raise yourself, grow your teams,
improve the infrastructure, enhance the community,
better the environment, improve everything. Improving
everything around us is the essence of leadership.
Leadership is not raising the bar and pushing people.

To be different, just be yourself

No two things are alike in nature. Not even the two
leaves of the same tree. You might wonder if it is true.
Yes, it looks alike because we cannot differentiate.
Be yourself. You will definitely be different.

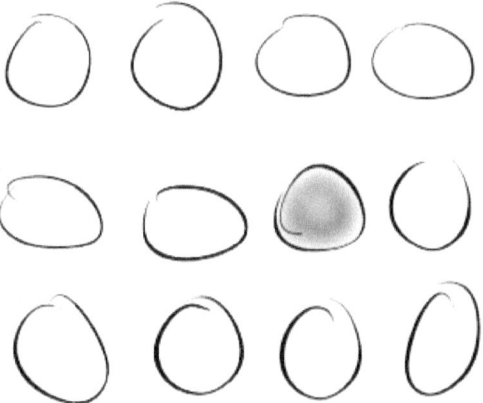

If you want to impress someone, choose yourself

If you can truly impress yourself, you will be truly content.
All the effort to impress others can lead to frustration.
Compete with your previous or existing self.

Increase your locus of impact not your locus of control

Our career progression is largely determined by how large our locus of control is, which is a management concept. A true leader, however, will increase the locus of impact.

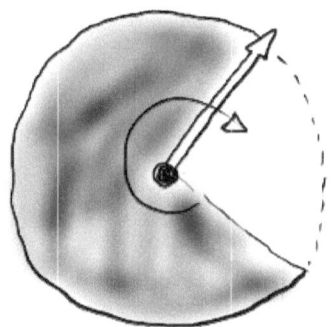

Diamonds don't shine in the dark

However good we are we need to be in the right environment. Without light a diamond will be as dull as the darkness around it. We need a stimulus, a ray of light to glow.

If something comes to you by itself, perhaps you are at a lower level

Things happen when we put in our efforts. If we aspire for things to come to us perhaps, we are at the wrong level, a lower level of energy. We need to get things done and not get things.

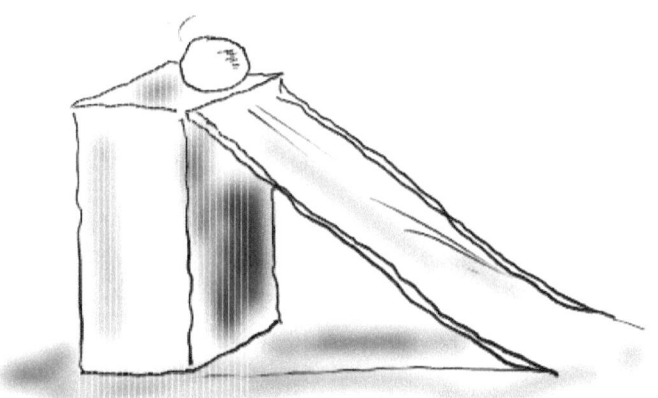

Plan B is for action only and not for outcomes

A typical approach is to have a plan B for a project plan or an important activity. It is important to realise that the plan B is for the action part of the plan. The ambition should not have a plan B.

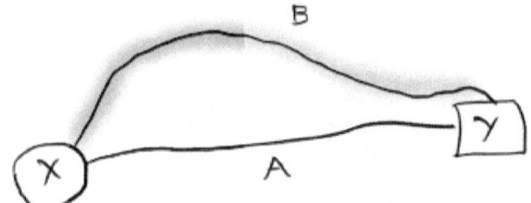

Leaders discuss advantages and disadvantages while managers talk about good and bad

When we align our value system the leader has achieved a great deal of success. The team has synergy by design. When we are behaving as managers and operating at a much lower level, we discuss good and bad things of a project.

Smart risk taking is about results and not actions

While we find some people are seemingly very good at 'risk-taking' it is something to understand. The risk is only in the outcome, the results but never in the action.

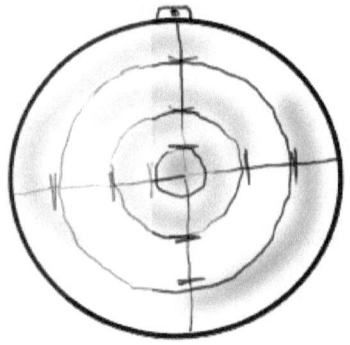

Question more answers than answer more questions

A lot of money is spent in finding answers to questions. Traditionally we are trained to solve problems than finding questions. Success is in finding the right question to answer.

Success is a hindsight thing

A lot of times we talk about success and it feels good. But remember it is always in hindsight. One can never say I am going to feel success tomorrow, next week etc. It is always a thing of the past.

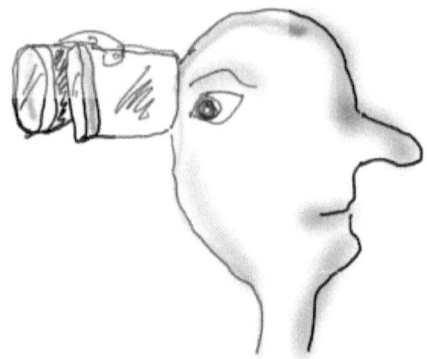

The past should be used to make a map, not a plan

Our experiences help us do better in the future. But it is not guaranteed nor automatic. Our experiences should be like a map. When we plan, we can use the experience of where we have been and what we got or didn't get there. Past experience should not limit the future journey but enhance it.

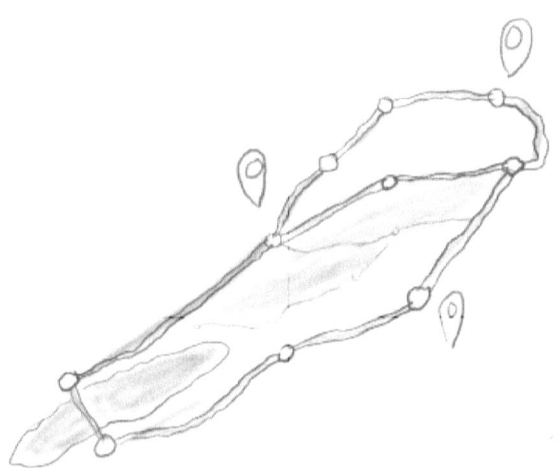

What is true and what is the truth, are not always the same thing

Assume a Rubik's cube is on a table. Every angle you see the cube from, gives you a 'view' which is true. This is not the entire truth, the whole cube, as you are missing some part of the cube, irrespective of the angle you take.

Intention gets your journey going, Decision sets your direction, Actions gets the outcomes

Intention is the key to start a journey. With intention there is an expectation. Action takes us from intention to expectation. Decisions are keys to choose your path of action. You still need to act to get there.

Procrastination is the gap between your mind and your heart

Good plans are made with good intentions, mediocre ones are made with good knowledge only. When what you wish and what you want are not the same, procrastination sets in. Then the mind asks you to do something while the heart wonders if you should really do it.

 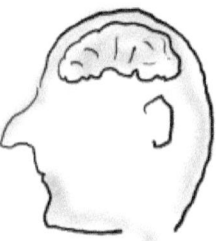

We all need wake up calls

We all certainly need wake up calls. It is needed so that we don't miss opportunities. Or it could save us from trouble. The wakeup call can be raised by us internally, powerful but rare. The wake up coming from outside is asynchronous, will not consider our preparedness or readiness to face it. In the end we get to face it.

Change is life;
Rate of change is growth

Observing living objects will tell us that as long as something is 'alive' it keeps changing. A plant which is alive grows new leaves, flowers and fruits, sheds old ones and keeps alive. Rate of change can be positive or negative. Rate of change implies progress if it is positive. Else the end is not far, if it is negative growth.

Fears are learnt

Psychology tells us today that we are born with two fears –
fear of falling and fear of loud sound. That means the rest is
more or less learnt. If we can learn something, we can also
unlearn something. Fear stops us from our full self. It prevents
us from trying. Do you want to unlearn your fears?

Risk is in the reward

People say you have to choose between options considering
the risk and reward. This is true especially in uncertain
situations. The fact is that the risk is in the reward.
They are two sides of the same coin. We need to take
our chances. Being safe is being without change.

It seems impossible – till you find a way

As children we were mesmerised by magic shows. As adults we are still at awe but somewhere, we know it is a trick. The disbelief of 'how on earth this can happen' lingers on. The day we know how the magic trick is done; we will know that what seemed impossible is possible.

ABRACADABRA!

If you just try, you will surprise yourself

Many a times for whatever reasons we stop ourselves from moving forward because we don't take action. One of the important reasons we don't take action is we are not confident of taking a certain action. The reasons for the lack of confidence can be many but the inhibition to try is the reason for not making progress. Trying can surprise you positively. Try, that's the best success for the moment.

Think different, more importantly act different

Thought and action are related. We can act what we think.
But before we can act different, we need to think different.
We need to think different so that we can be better.
Thought precedes action, but action yields result.

Be child-like, not childish

Among other things children are very creative. The most common reason quoted for this is that the children are not conditioned yet. For us, the grown-ups, to be creative as we were as children is possible. For that we need to have an enormous child-like curiosity. This curiosity will keep our minds open and closes the gates of inhibition.

Don't respect failure more than yourself

Failure is considered negative in general. The glorification of failure is misplaced. We don't need to fail fast. We don't need to fail, if we understand what we call failure as. If you define it as a gap between plan versus actual, it becomes much more reasonable way to deal with.

Today's future is tomorrow's past

We need to prepare for the future. The horizons of future can vary on the topic we are preparing for the future. Some can be nearby, and some can be far off today. But the key fact to recognise that today's future, tomorrow is the present one day later. We need to keep it in mind that the future will also arrive, sooner or later.

Be in the top 3 in what you do

Finding your sweet spot is very important. This ensures that your path to success is that of least resistance. It is normal that we meet success sometimes and sometimes not. But the key is to be in the top three in whatever we do.

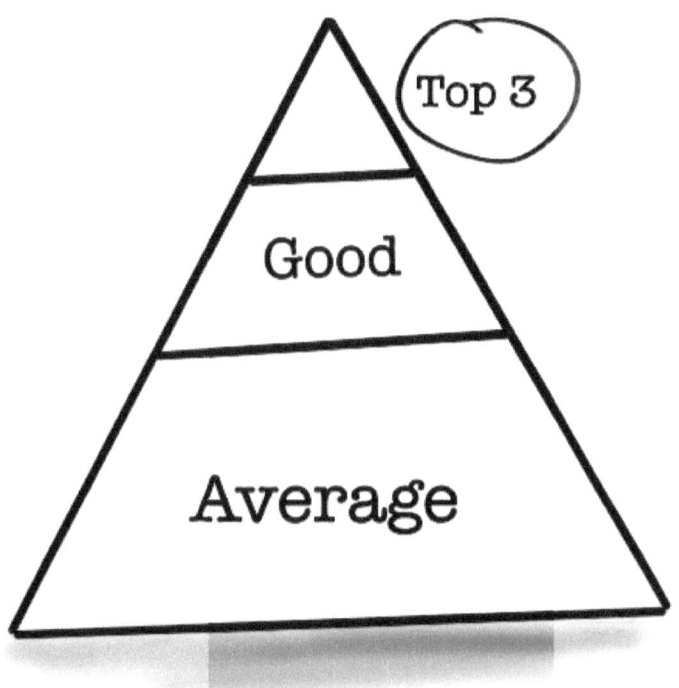

Motivation is our own business

Zig Ziglar advises that like bathe daily we need to motivate ourselves daily. It is up to us to pull our own weight. A car has to move itself forward along with its passengers. An autonomous car will move by itself even when no one is there. We need to find our own ways and means to motivate ourselves, to propel in the direction we have chosen.

Don't be afraid to be you

A common problem is that we often get modulated by what we are told about us. Over the years cumulatively we tend to be someone who we are not. Once we realise that perhaps we are not being who we are, we worry to even acknowledge that fact. We worry to be who we really are. Should we be afraid to be who we really are?

Patience for the right things is a virtue

Patience can be a double-edged sword. Patience can be a very philosophical concept. But patience can also be a deterrent to take decisions and take action. So, having patience for the right things at the right time to the right extent, that is a virtue.

Teamwork never goes out of fashion

As we become better individuals, we need to remember everything significant can be achieved as a team only. Whatever be the technological progress, we need a coherent set of people called a team to make things happen. So be a good team member is an important aspect of being a better person.

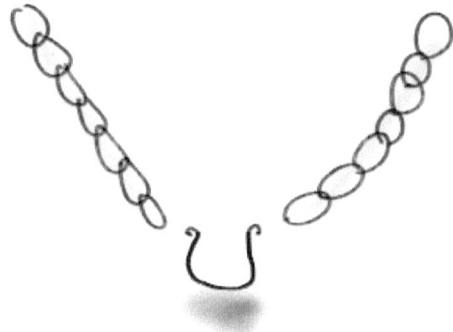

Keep an eye on your habits

Good habits or bad ones are with each of us. While it is good to have the habits, which helps us get better, we need to be aware of our bad habits. Many times, relinquishing bad habits can be more effective than developing good habits. Keep an eye on your habits.

Extraordinary Success is achieved by ordinary people with extraordinary determination

You will never see a seriously successful person with an easy past. Setbacks and hurdles are two things they would have overcome in plenty to get to a point of extraordinary success. The force behind their success is more often determination, much more than skill.

Don't stop having fun

When we enjoy something, we will 'know' we are having fun. Another indicator is that we will not realise how quickly time has flown. With these two indicators we will know we are having fun. Difficulties do not seem to be difficulties in such cases. The day we stop feeling one or both of the above we need to introspect.

ABOUT THE AUTHOR

Dr Sudeendra Koushik

Dr Koushik is a professional Innovator, worked across the world with accomplishments in technology, management and leadership. He consults for many fortune 500 companies and has enabled leadership and innovation culture in many organisation. Dr Koushik is also a keynote speaker and TEDx speaker.

www.ingramcontent.com/pod-product-compliance
Lightning Source LLC
Chambersburg PA
CBHW030521220526
45463CB00007B/2659